ANIMAL Infographics

Chris Oxlade

Raintree
Chicago, Illinois

an imprint of Capstone Global Library, LLC
Chicago, Illinois

To contact Capstone Global Library, please call 800-747-4992, or visit our web site www.capstonepub.com

Edited by Rebecca Rissman, Dan Nunn, and John-Paul Wilkins
Designed by Philippa Jenkins
Original illustrations © Capstone Global Library Ltd 2014
Illustrations by HL Studios
Picture research by Elizabeth Alexander
Production by Vicki Fitzgerald
Originated by Capstone Global Library Ltd
Printed in the United States of America in
North Mankato, MN. 042014 008185RP

Library of Congress Cataloging-in-Publication Data
Oxlade, Chris.
Animals / Chris Oxlade.
pages cm.—(Infographics)
Includes bibliographical references and index.
ISBN 978-1-4109-6216-4 (hardback)—ISBN 978-1-4109-6221-8 (paperback) 1. Graphic methods—Juvenile literature. 2. Charts, diagrams, etc.—Juvenile literature. 3. Animals—Juvenile literature. I. Title.
QA90.O95 2014
590.72'8—dc23 2013012529

Acknowledgments
We would like to thank the following for permission to reproduce photographs: Capstone Global Library p. 4; Shutterstock pp. 4 (© M.Stasy, © Pakhnyushcha, © Stella Caraman, © Thomas Bethge).

We would like to thank Diana Bentley and Marla Conn for their invaluable help in the preparation of this book.

Metric Conversions

Length and Distance
1 centimeter = 0.4 inch
1 foot = 0.3 meter
1 kilometer = 0.6 mile

Speed
1 kilometer per hour = 0.6 mile per hour

Weight
1 kilogram = 2.2 pounds
1 metric ton = 1.1 tons

1 centimeter
1 inch

CONTENTS

Some words are shown in bold, **like this**. You can find out what they mean by looking in the glossary.

ABOUT INFOGRAPHICS

An infographic is a picture that gives you information. Infographics can be graphs, charts, maps, or other sorts of pictures. The infographics in this book are about animals.

Infographics make information easier to understand. We see infographics all over the place, every day. They appear in books, in newspapers, on television, on web sites, on posters, and in advertisements.

Here is a simple infographic about pets. It shows the number of different pets in the United States.

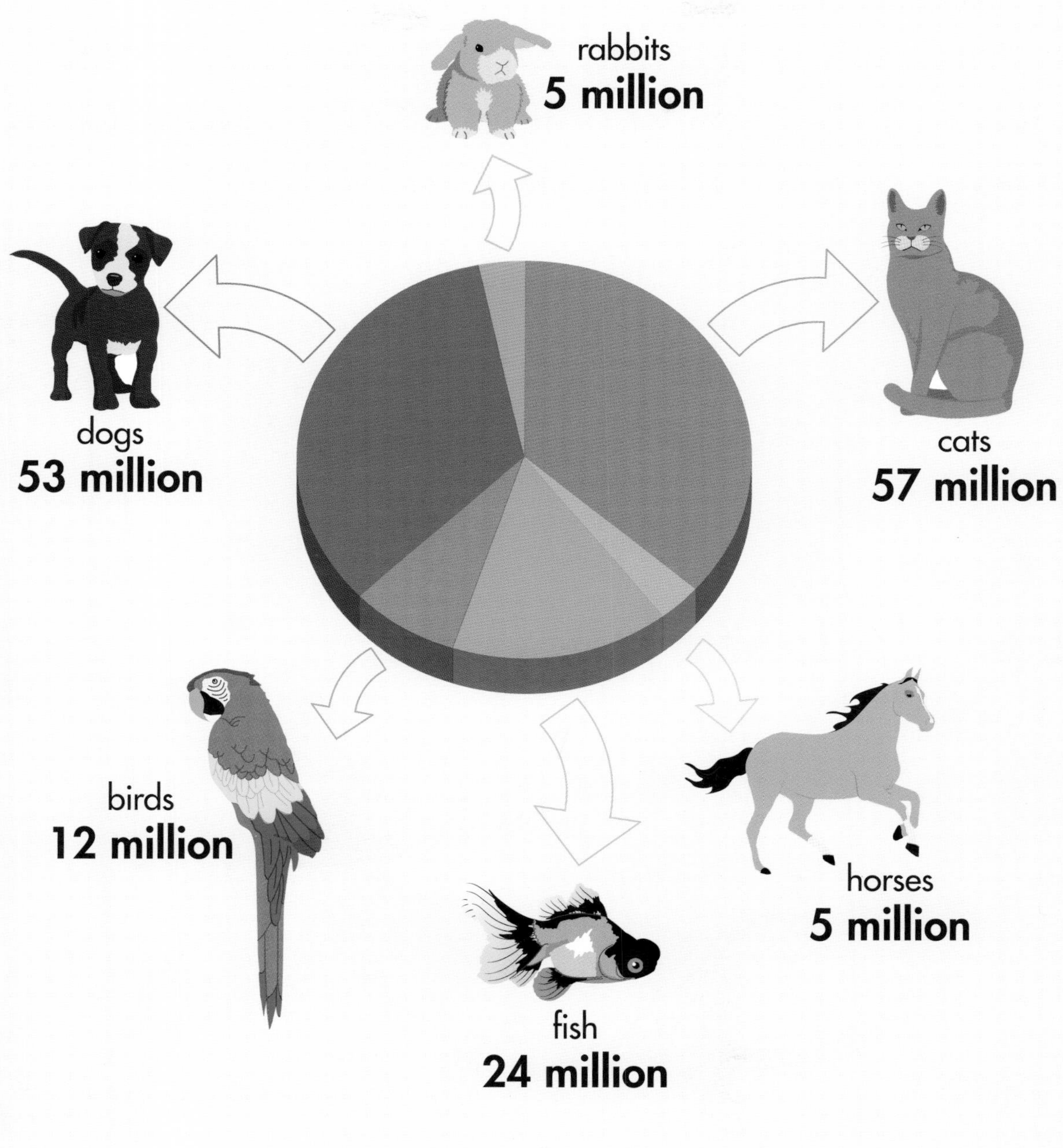
rabbits
5 million
dogs
53 million
cats
57 million
birds
12 million
horses
5 million
fish
24 million

SIZE AND SHAPE

Big animal facts

The blue whale and the African elephant are two of the world's biggest animals. These infographics present some amazing facts about them.

African elephant

height **12 feet** tall

weight **6.6 tons**

tusks up to **11.5 feet** long

trunk **8.2 feet** long

drinks **42 gallons** of water a day

Blue whale

length **98 feet**

can stay underwater for **1.5 hours**

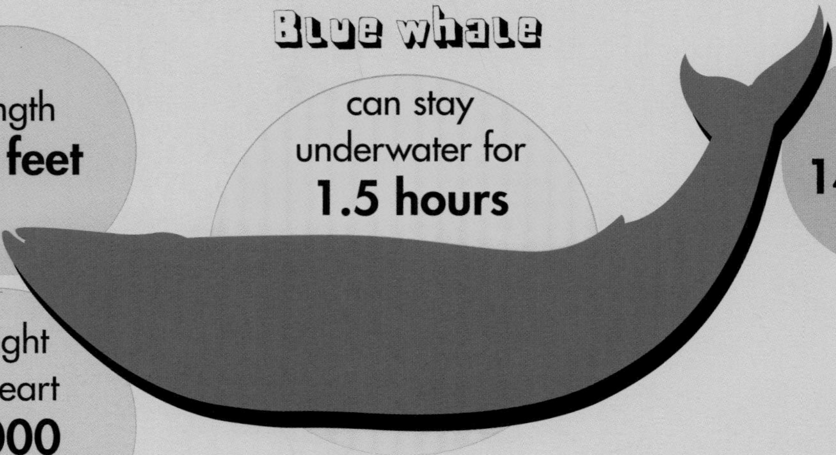

weight **145 tons**

weight of heart **2,000 pounds**

Comparing weights

How many elephants are equal to a blue whale? This chart compares the weights of different animals.

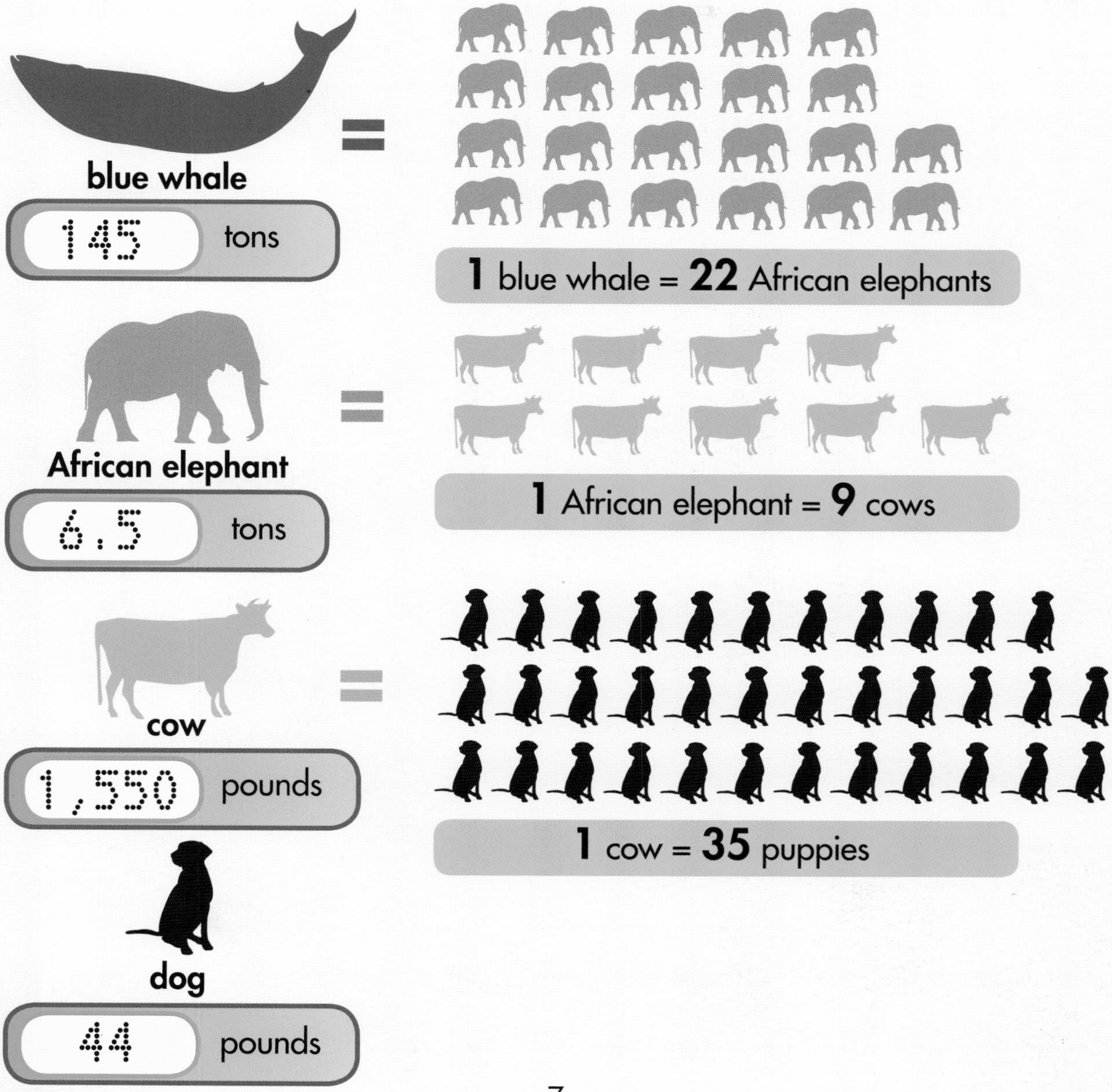
blue whale
145 tons
1 blue whale = 22 African elephants
African elephant
6.5 tons
1 African elephant = 9 cows
cow
1,550 pounds
1 cow = 35 puppies
dog
44 pounds

The biggest animals

We put animals into different groups, such as mammals and birds. This chart shows the biggest animals in different animal groups.

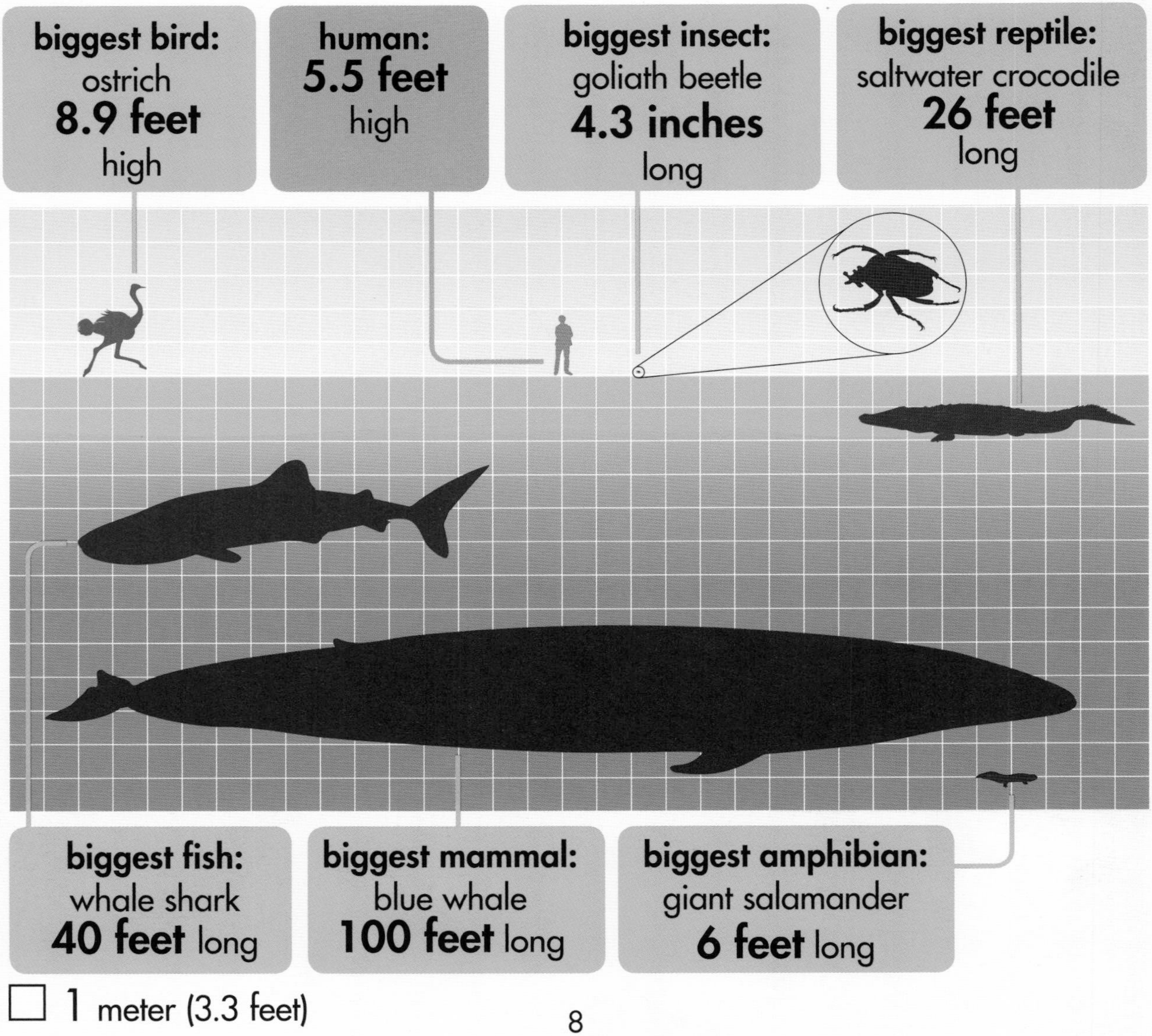

biggest bird: ostrich 8.9 feet high
human: 5.5 feet high
biggest insect: goliath beetle 4.3 inches long
biggest reptile: saltwater crocodile 26 feet long
biggest fish: whale shark 40 feet long
biggest mammal: blue whale 100 feet long
biggest amphibian: giant salamander 6 feet long
1 meter (3.3 feet)

The smallest animals

This chart shows you the smallest animals. You can see the size of each animal compared to an adult human's hand.

smallest reptile:
dwarf gecko
0.8 inch long

smallest amphibian:
forest-dwelling frog from Papua New Guinea
0.03 inch long

smallest insect:
fairy fly
0.0008 inch long

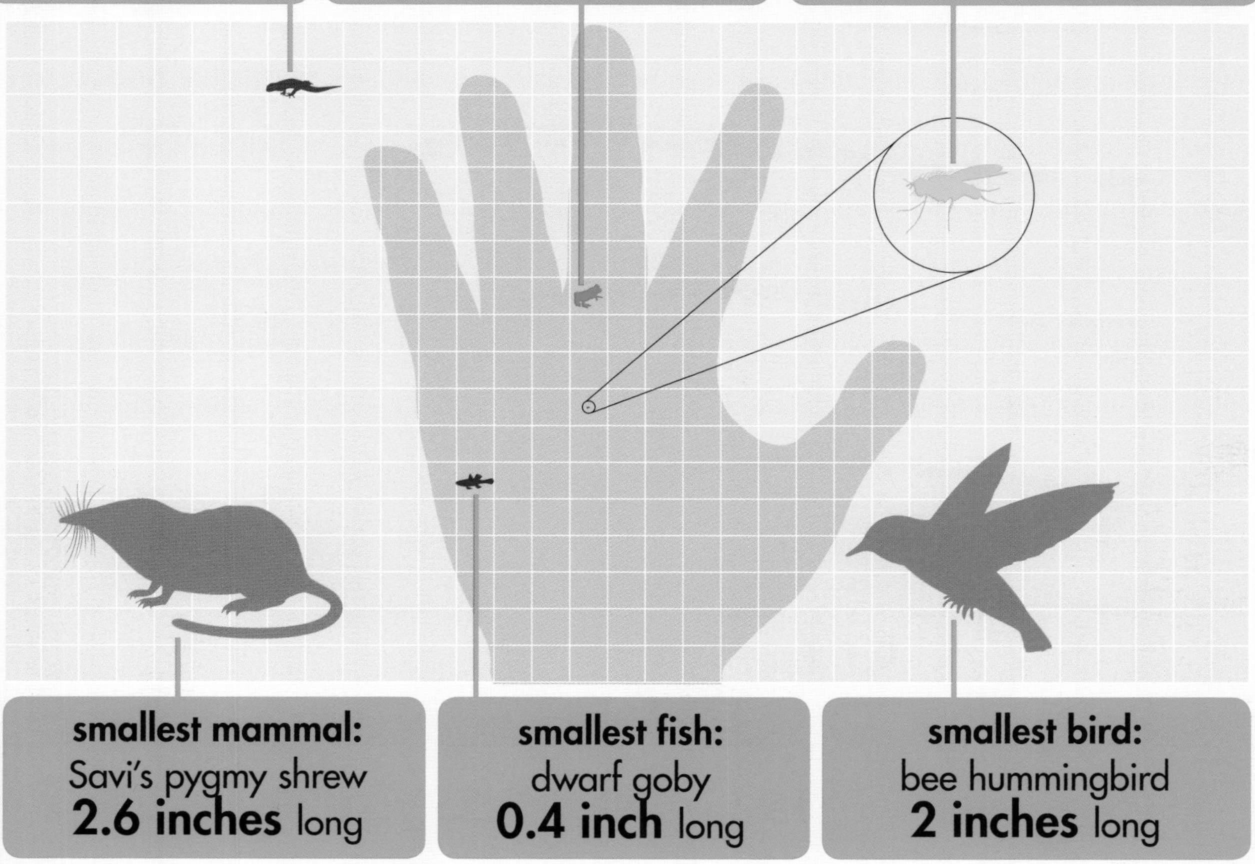

smallest mammal:
Savi's pygmy shrew
2.6 inches long

smallest fish:
dwarf goby
0.4 inch long

smallest bird:
bee hummingbird
2 inches long

□ 1 centimeter (0.4 inch)

The longest snakes

This bar chart shows the lengths of the five longest snakes in the world.

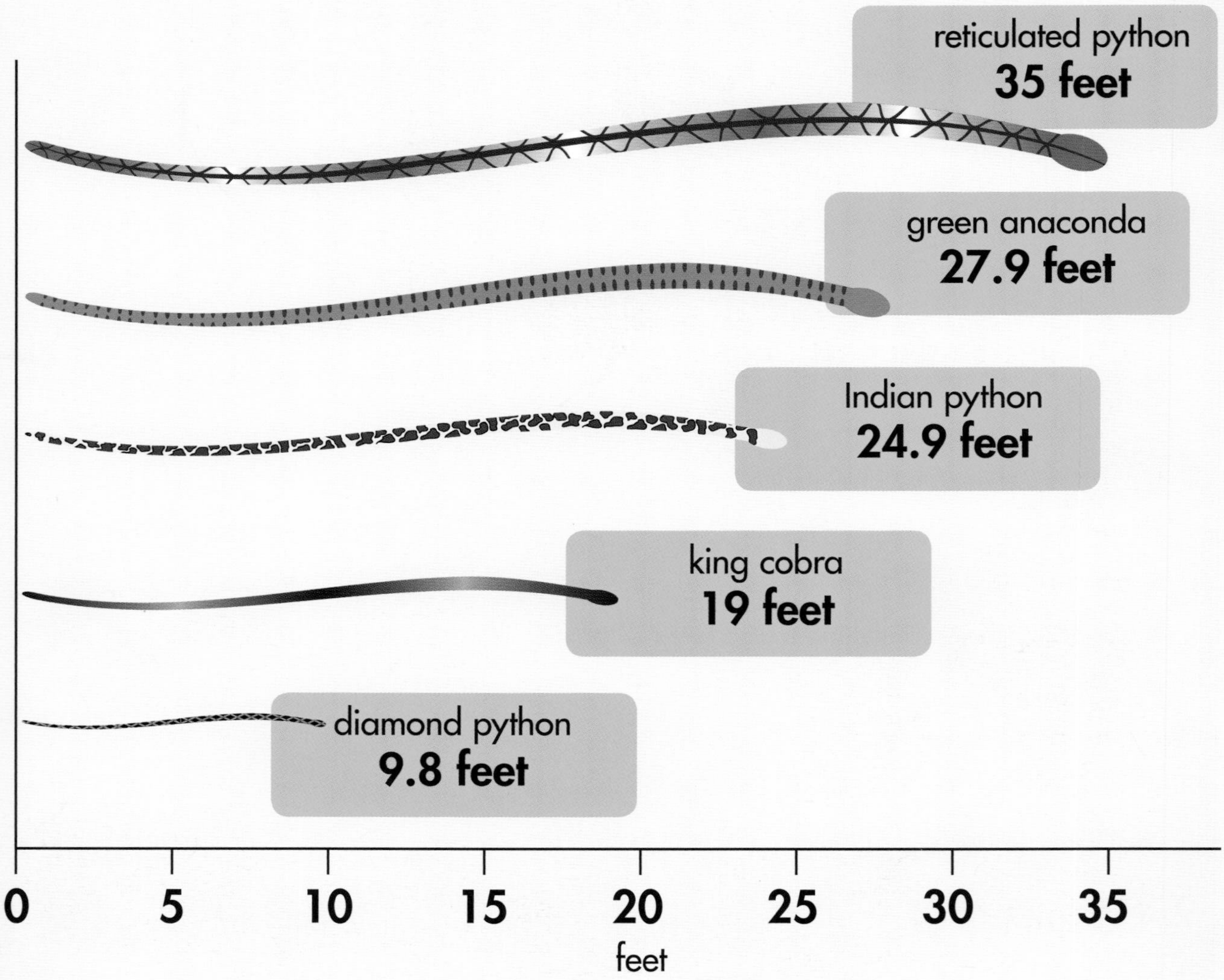
reticulated python
35 feet
green anaconda
27.9 feet
Indian python
24.9 feet
king cobra
19 feet
diamond python
9.8 feet
0
5
10
15
20
25
30
35
feet

Big insects

The biggest insects are very big! This chart shows the sizes of some of the biggest insects.

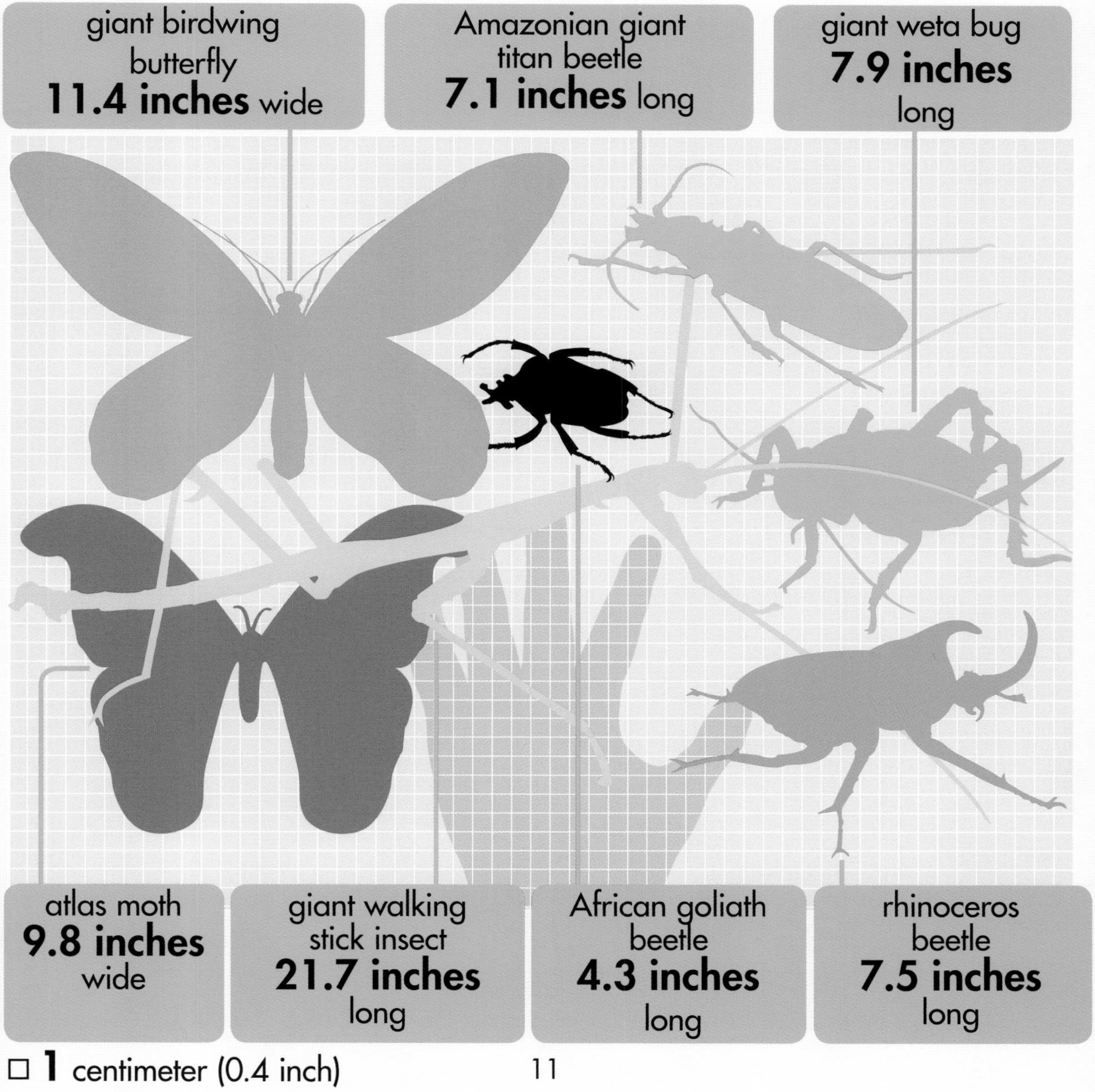
giant birdwing butterfly
11.4 inches wide
Amazonian giant titan beetle
7.1 inches long
giant weta bug
7.9 inches long
atlas moth
9.8 inches wide
giant walking stick insect
21.7 inches long
African goliath beetle
4.3 inches long
rhinoceros beetle
7.5 inches long
□ **1** centimeter (0.4 inch)

MOVING ANIMALS

Fastest on land

This chart shows the top speeds of some of the fastest animals on land.

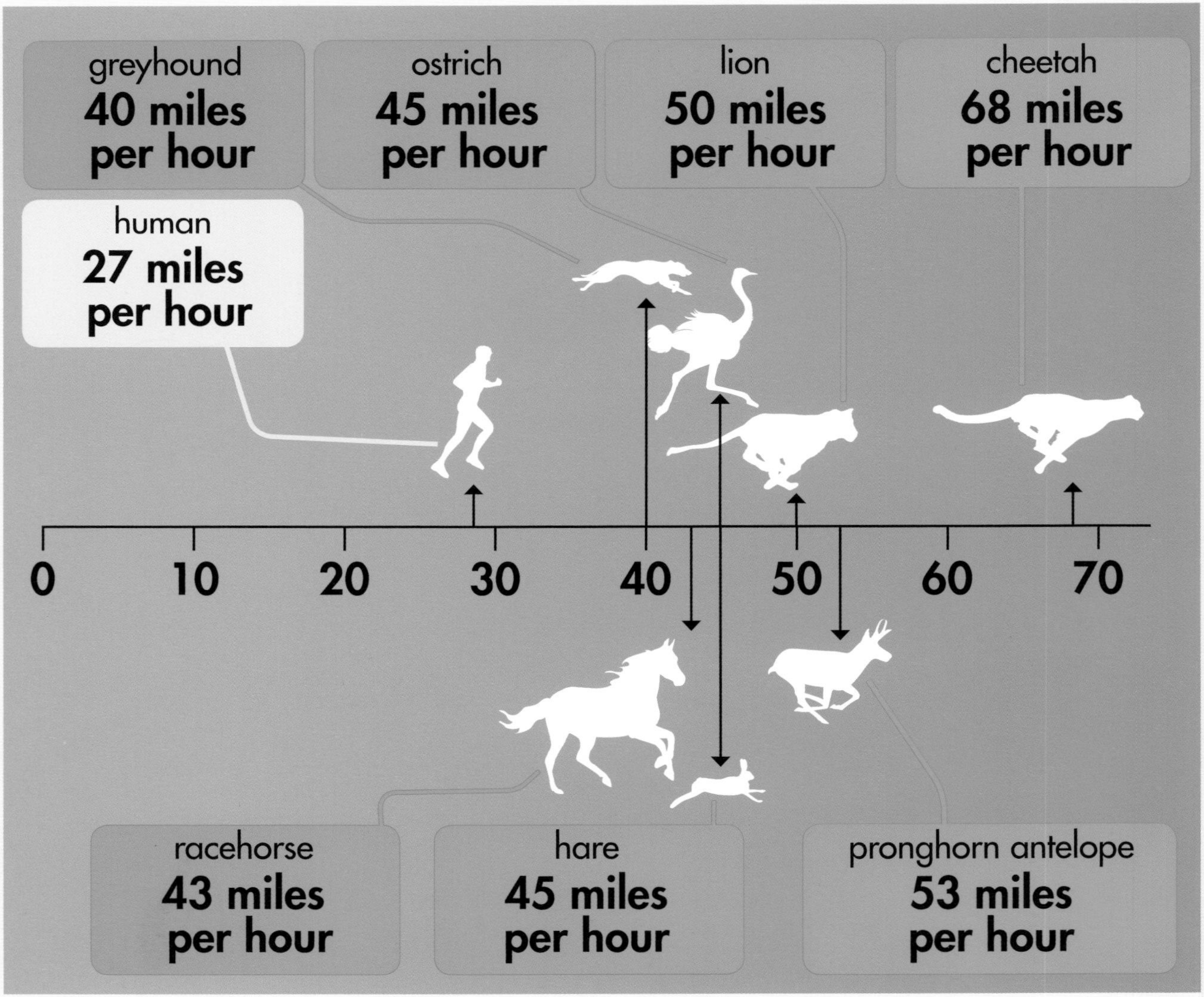
greyhound
40 miles per hour
ostrich
45 miles per hour
lion
50 miles per hour
cheetah
68 miles per hour
human
27 miles per hour
0
10
20
30
40
50
60
70
racehorse
43 miles per hour
hare
45 miles per hour
pronghorn antelope
53 miles per hour

The fastest in the air

This chart shows some of the fastest fliers in the air.

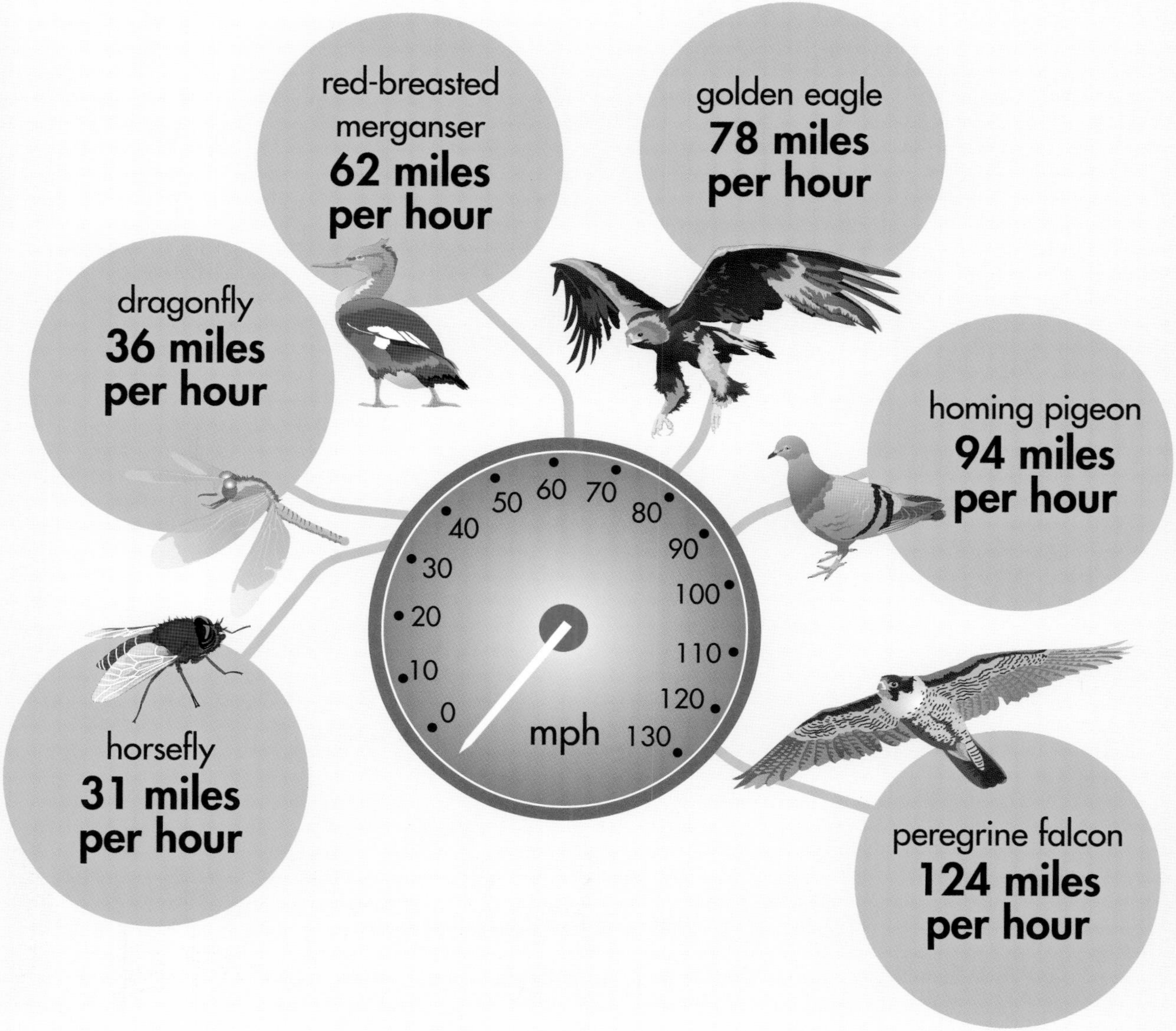
red-breasted merganser
62 miles per hour
golden eagle
78 miles per hour
dragonfly
36 miles per hour
homing pigeon
94 miles per hour
0
10
20
30
40
50
60
70
80
90
100
110
120
130
mph
horsefly
31 miles per hour
peregrine falcon
124 miles per hour

Slow animals

Some animals move very slowly. This chart shows how many minutes and seconds some of the slowest animals take to travel 1 meter (3.3 feet).

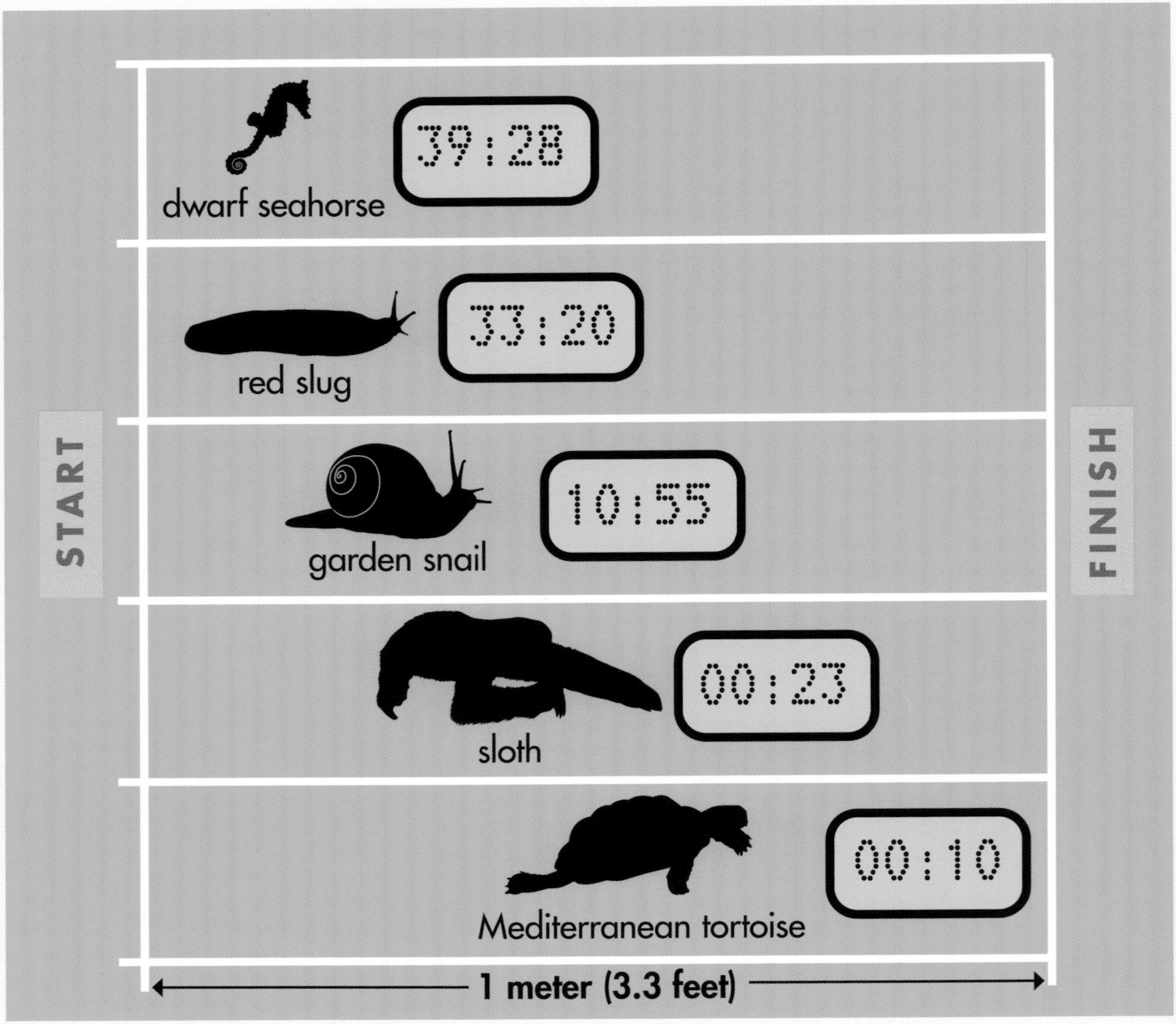

START
FINISH
39:28
dwarf seahorse
33:20
red slug
10:55
garden snail
00:23
sloth
00:10
Mediterranean tortoise
1 meter (3.3 feet)

High jump and long jump

Some animals can jump amazingly high and far. This chart shows some of the best animal jumpers, compared to the best human jumpers.

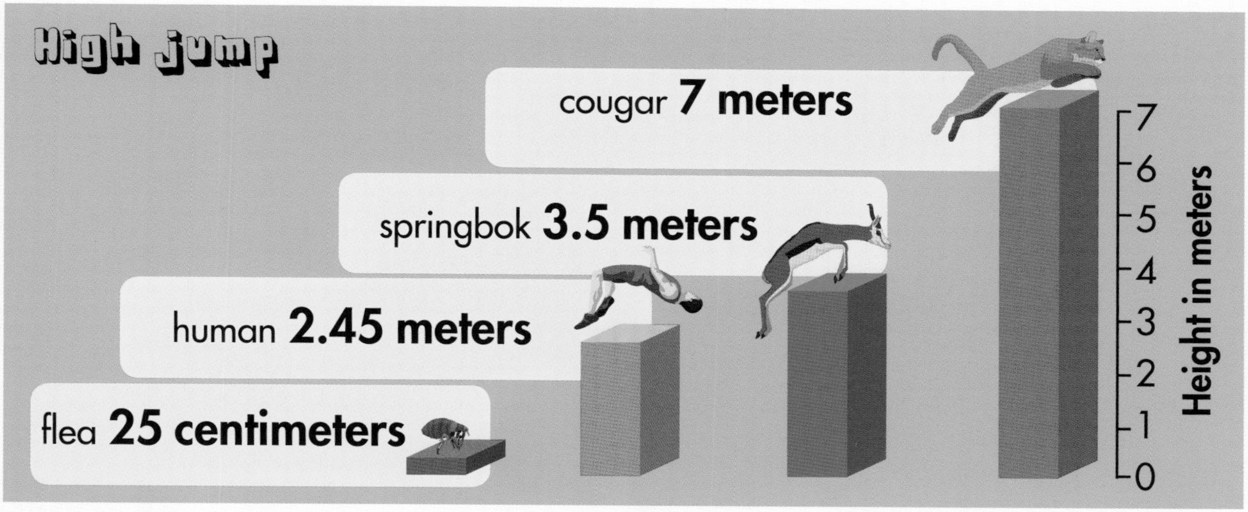

High jump
cougar 7 meters
springbok 3.5 meters
human 2.45 meters
flea 25 centimeters
0
1
2
3
4
5
6
7
Height in meters

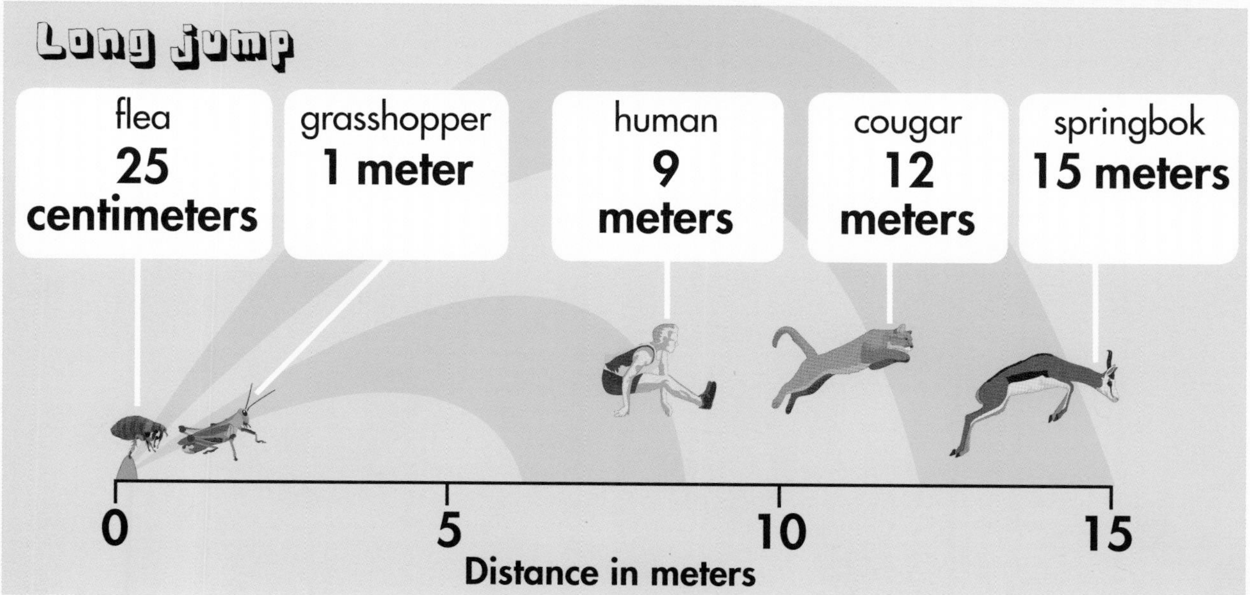

Long jump
flea 25 centimeters
grasshopper 1 meter
human 9 meters
cougar 12 meters
springbok 15 meters
0
5
10
15
Distance in meters

Biggest eyes

Some animals have enormous eyes. This chart shows the widths of the biggest animal eyes, with a human eye to compare them with.

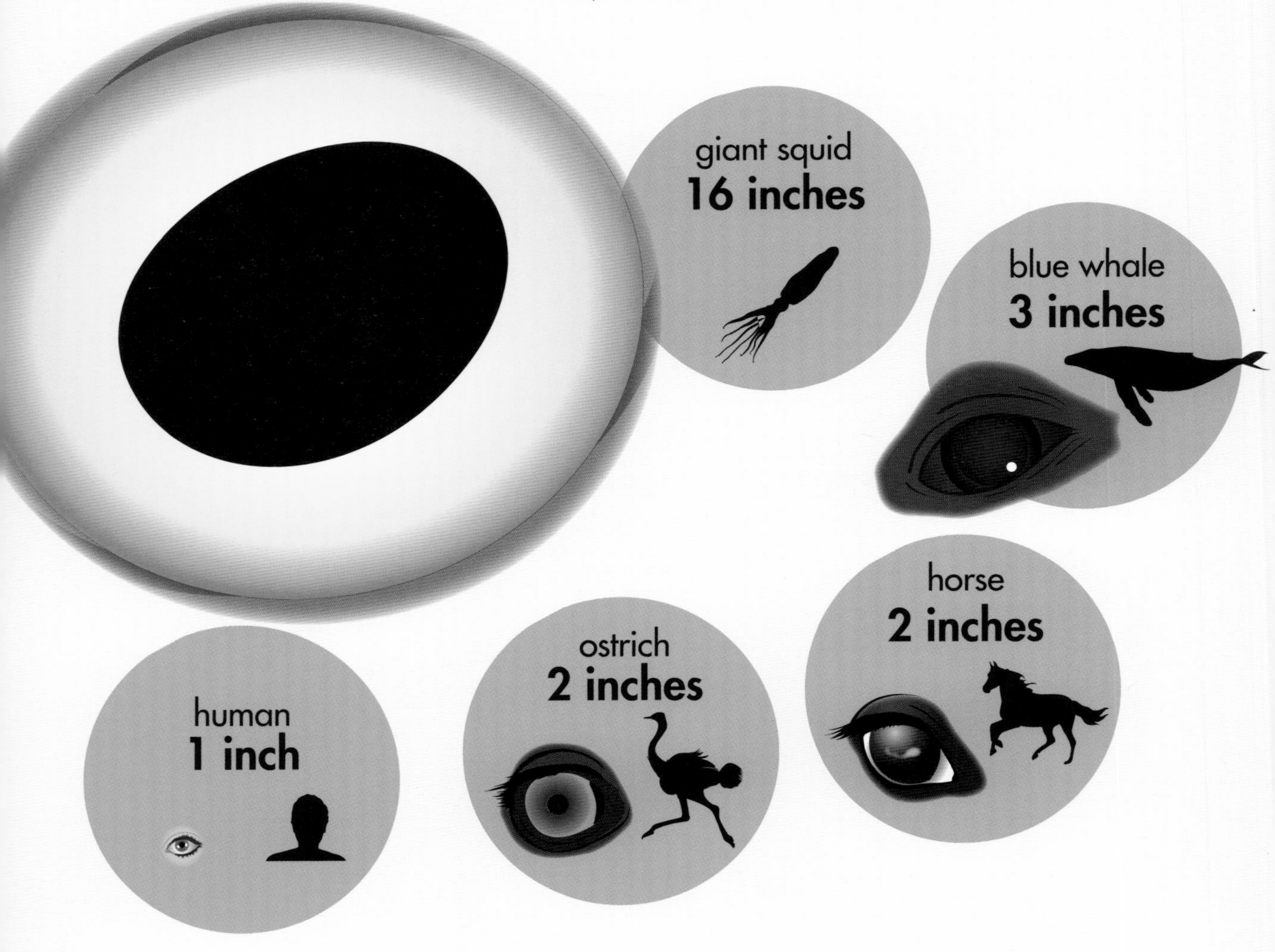
giant squid
16 inches
blue whale
3 inches
horse
2 inches
ostrich
2 inches
human
1 inch

The biggest teeth

This chart shows the lengths of the biggest animal teeth. They make human teeth look tiny!

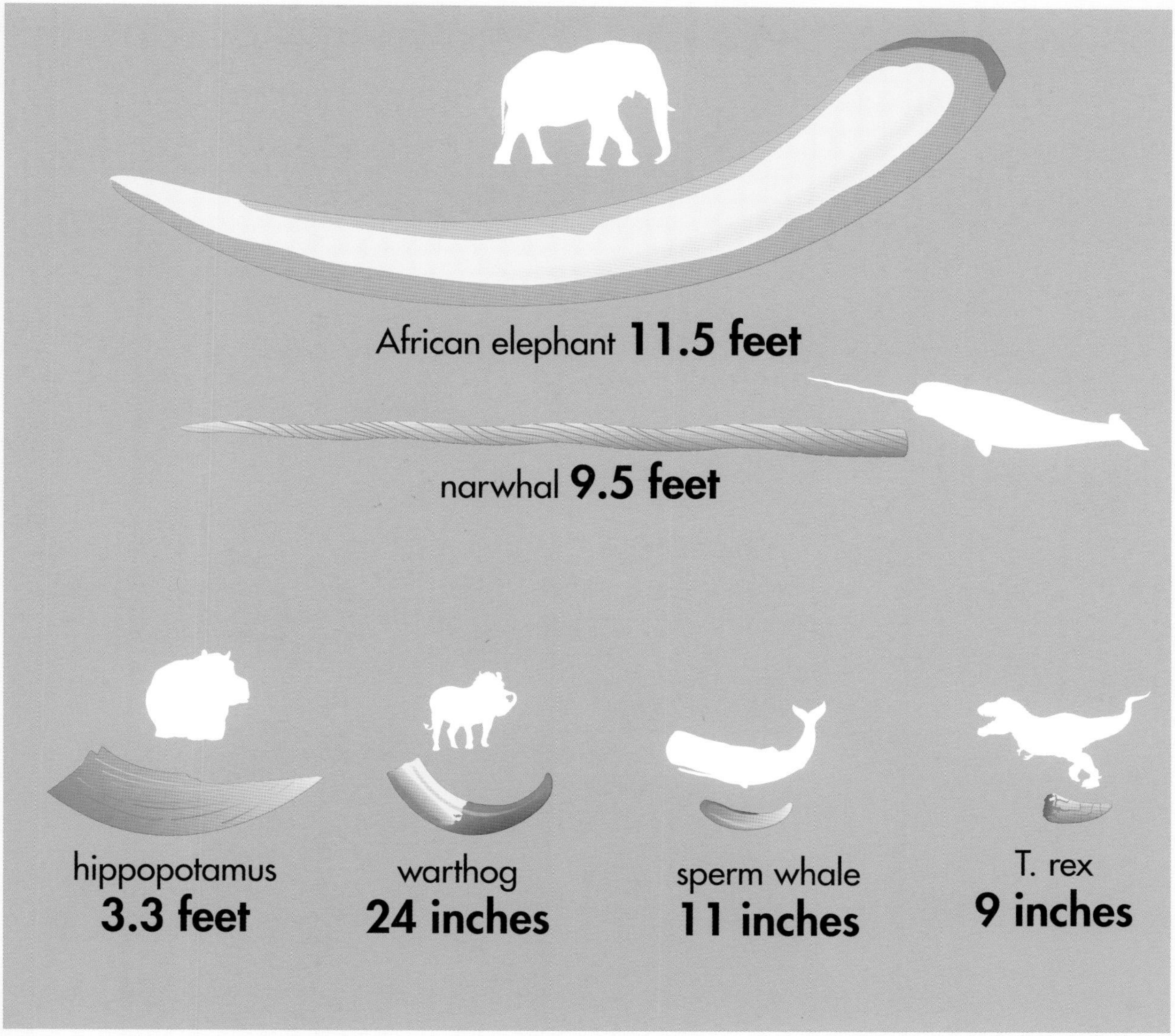
African elephant **11.5 feet**
narwhal **9.5 feet**
hippopotamus **3.3 feet**
warthog **24 inches**
sperm whale **11 inches**
T. rex **9 inches**

NUMBERS OF ANIMALS

Food chains

Animals have to eat plants and other animals to live. Animal diets can be shown in diagrams called food chains. This food-chain pyramid shows how many other animals or plants need to live in the same place for each animal to survive.

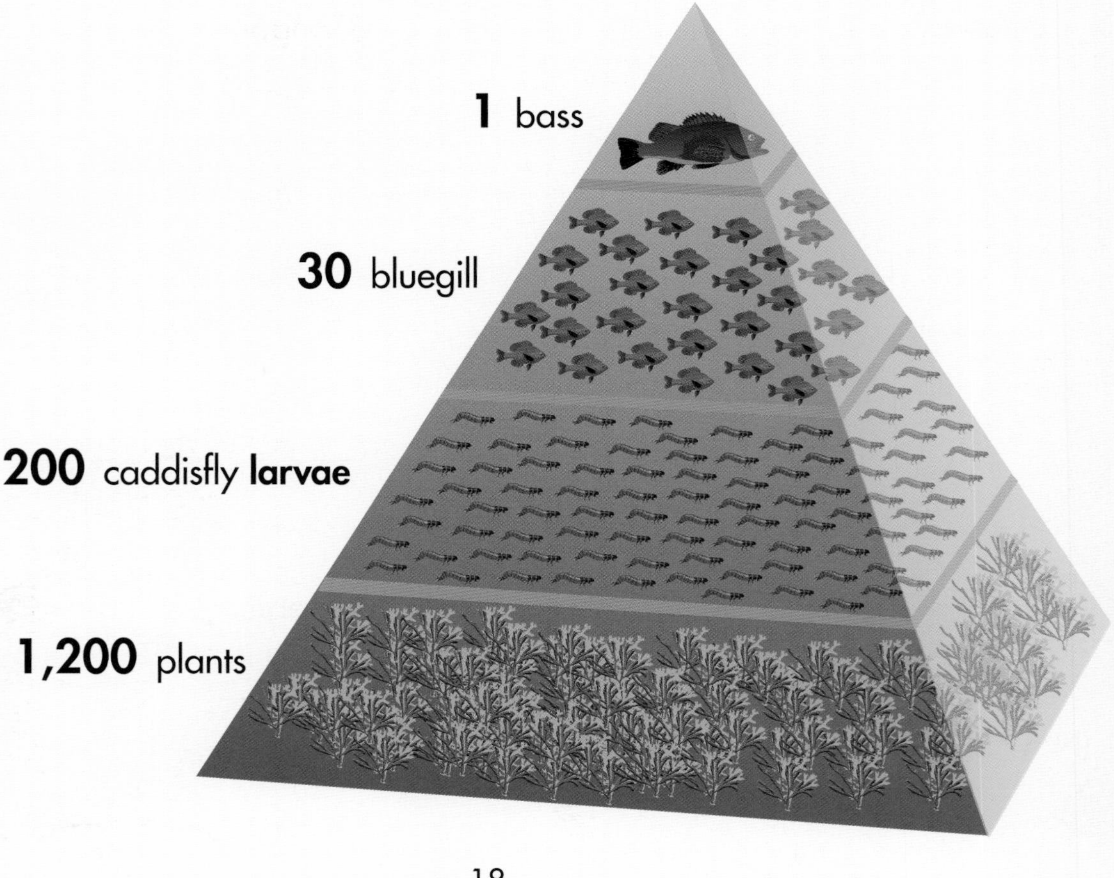

1 bass
30 bluegill
200 caddisfly **larvae**
1,200 plants

Animals in danger

Many animals around the world are hunted so much that there are almost none left. Or their habitats are being lost. This chart shows some of these **endangered** animals.

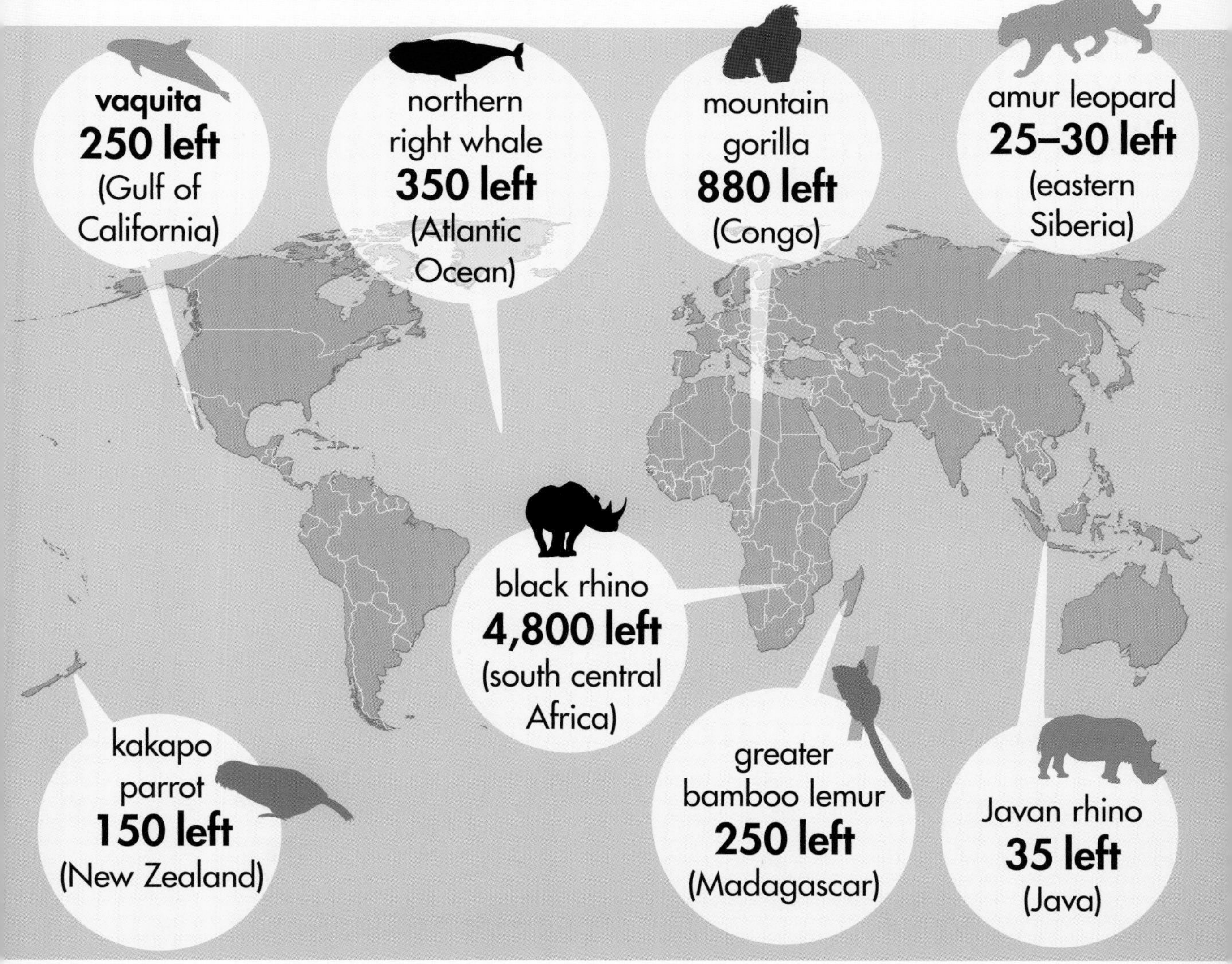

vaquita
250 left
(Gulf of California)
northern right whale
350 left
(Atlantic Ocean)
mountain gorilla
880 left
(Congo)
amur leopard
25–30 left
(eastern Siberia)
black rhino
4,800 left
(south central Africa)
kakapo parrot
150 left
(New Zealand)
greater bamboo lemur
250 left
(Madagascar)
Javan rhino
35 left
(Java)

ANIMAL LIFE SPANS

Animals that live the longest

This chart shows you how long different kinds of animals live.

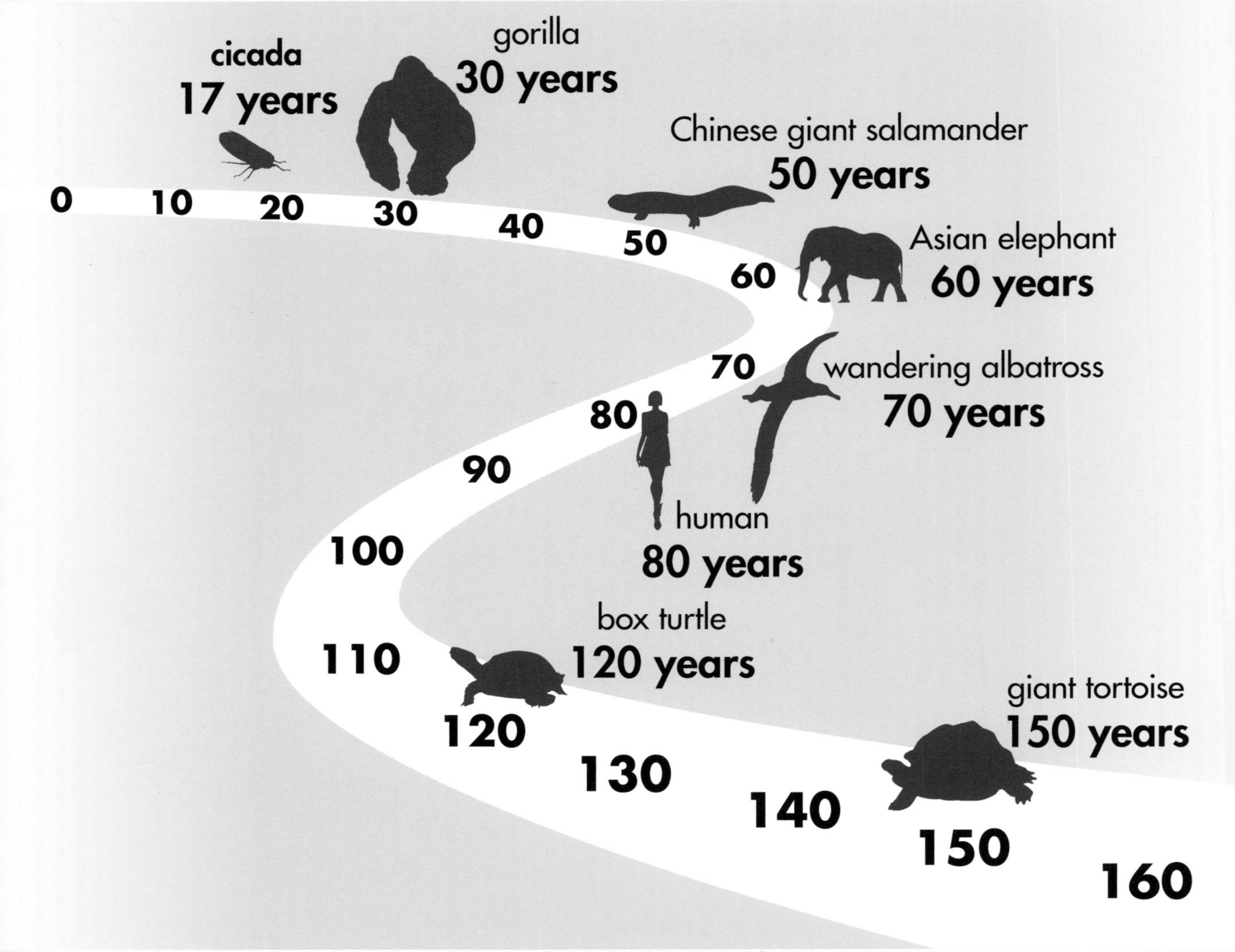

cicada
17 years
gorilla
30 years
Chinese giant salamander
50 years
Asian elephant
60 years
wandering albatross
70 years
human
80 years
box turtle
120 years
giant tortoise
150 years
0
10
20
30
40
50
60
70
80
90
100
110
120
130
140
150
160

Short lives

Some animals live only for a few months. Some only live for a few days! This calendar shows how long five animals, all born on January 1, would live.

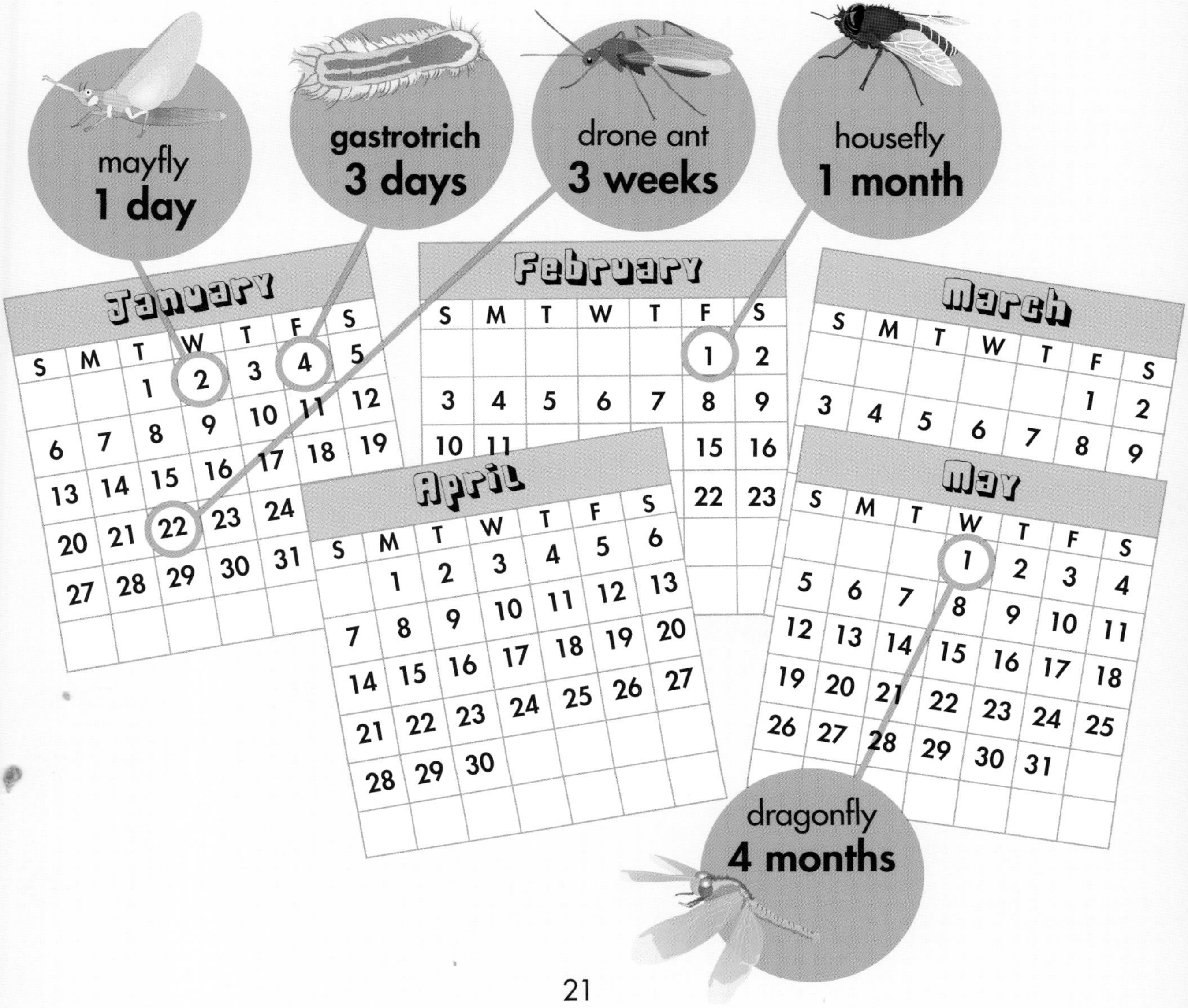
mayfly
1 day
gastrotrich
3 days
drone ant
3 weeks
housefly
1 month
January
February
March
April
May
dragonfly
4 months

LIFE CYCLES

The life cycle of an animal can show how the animal is born, lives, and has babies. Here are the life cycles of a frog and a butterfly.

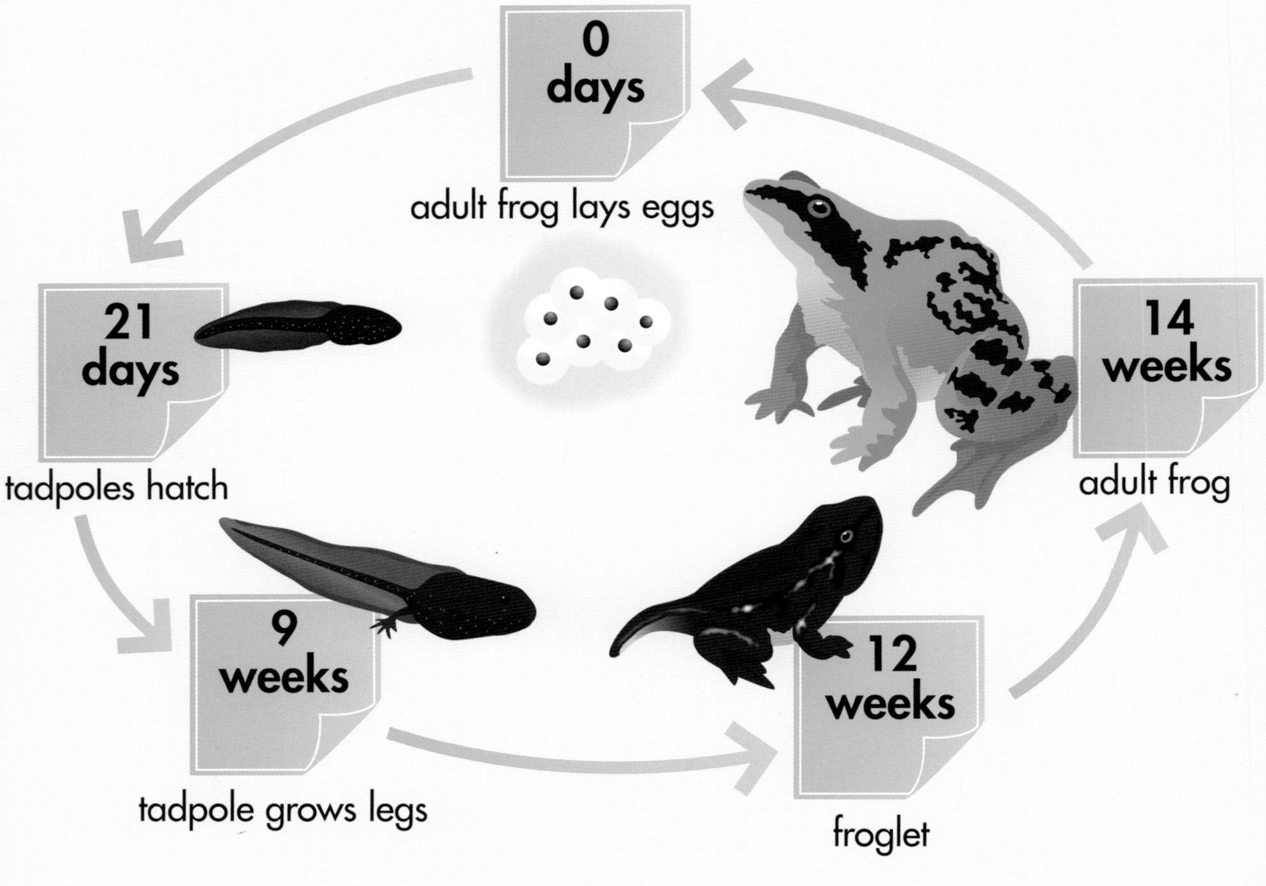

0 days
adult frog lays eggs
21 days
tadpoles hatch
9 weeks
tadpole grows legs
12 weeks
froglet
14 weeks
adult frog

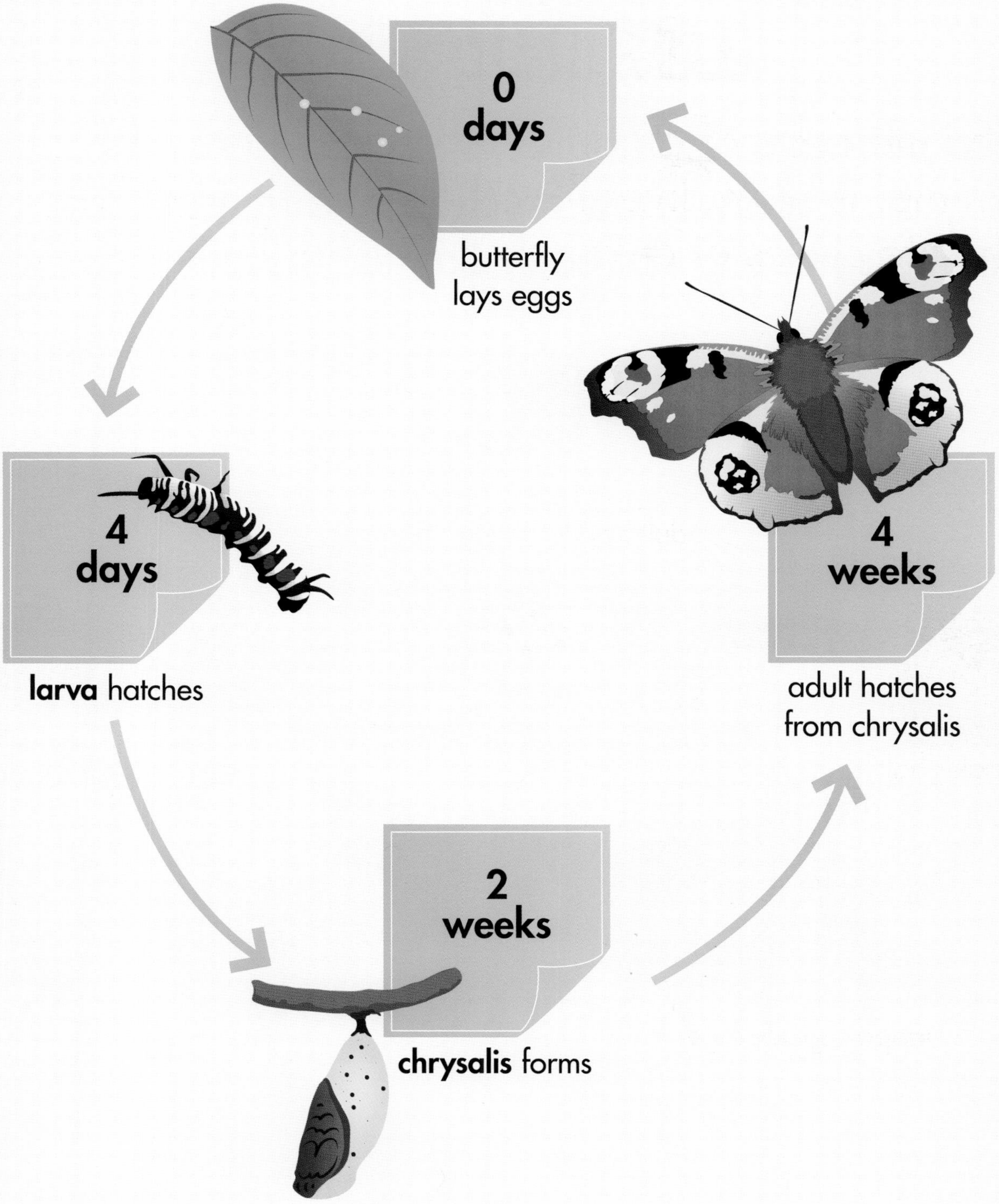
0
days
butterfly
lays eggs
4
days
larva hatches
2
weeks
chrysalis forms
4
weeks
adult hatches
from chrysalis

ANIMAL FOOD

Big dinners

This chart shows how much food different animals have to eat each day to stay alive.

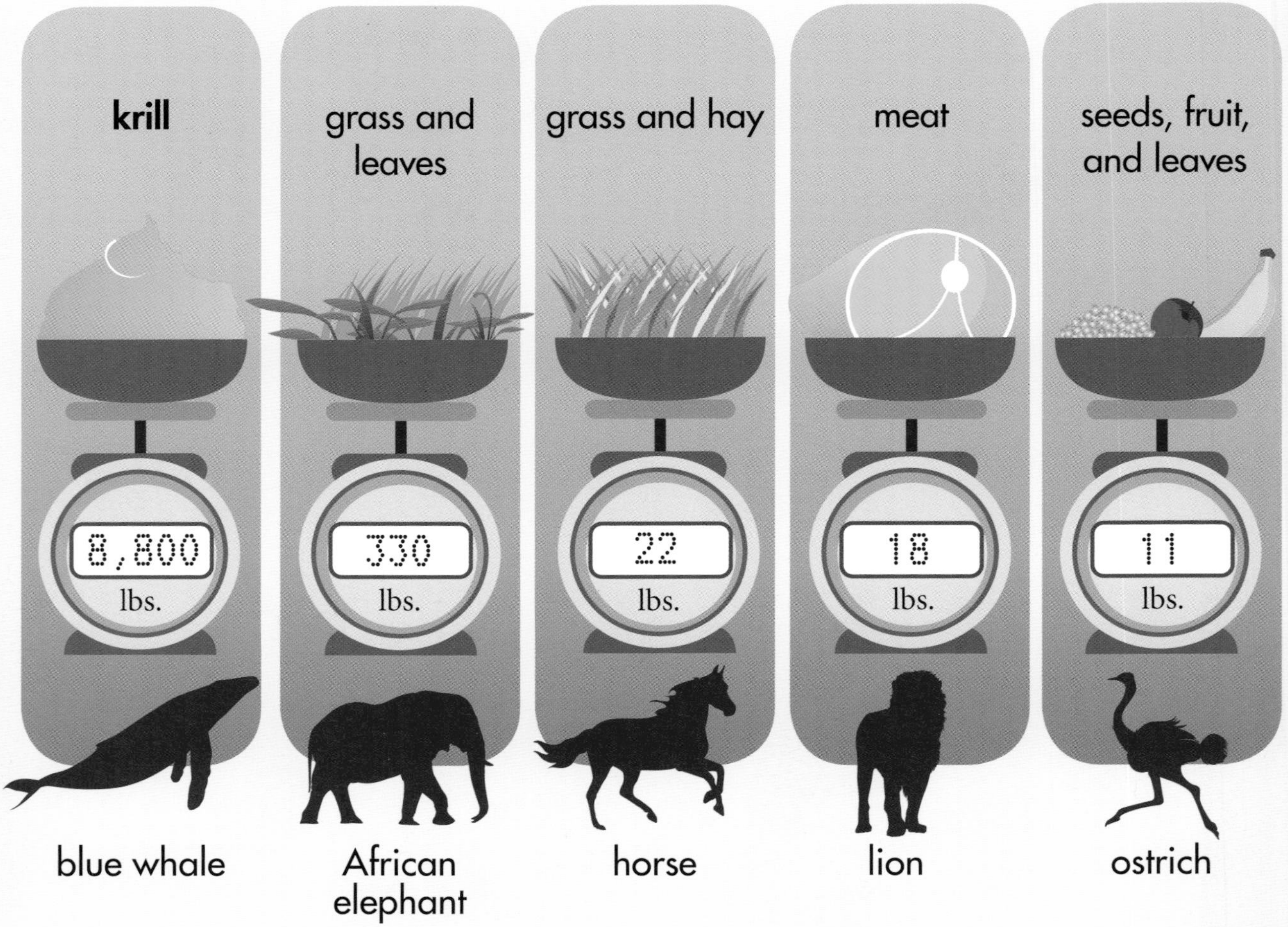
krill
grass and leaves
grass and hay
meat
seeds, fruit, and leaves
8,800
lbs.
330
lbs.
22
lbs.
18
lbs.
11
lbs.
blue whale
African elephant
horse
lion
ostrich

What eats what

This chart shows what animals eat plants and other animals. It is called a food web. This food web is for a forest.

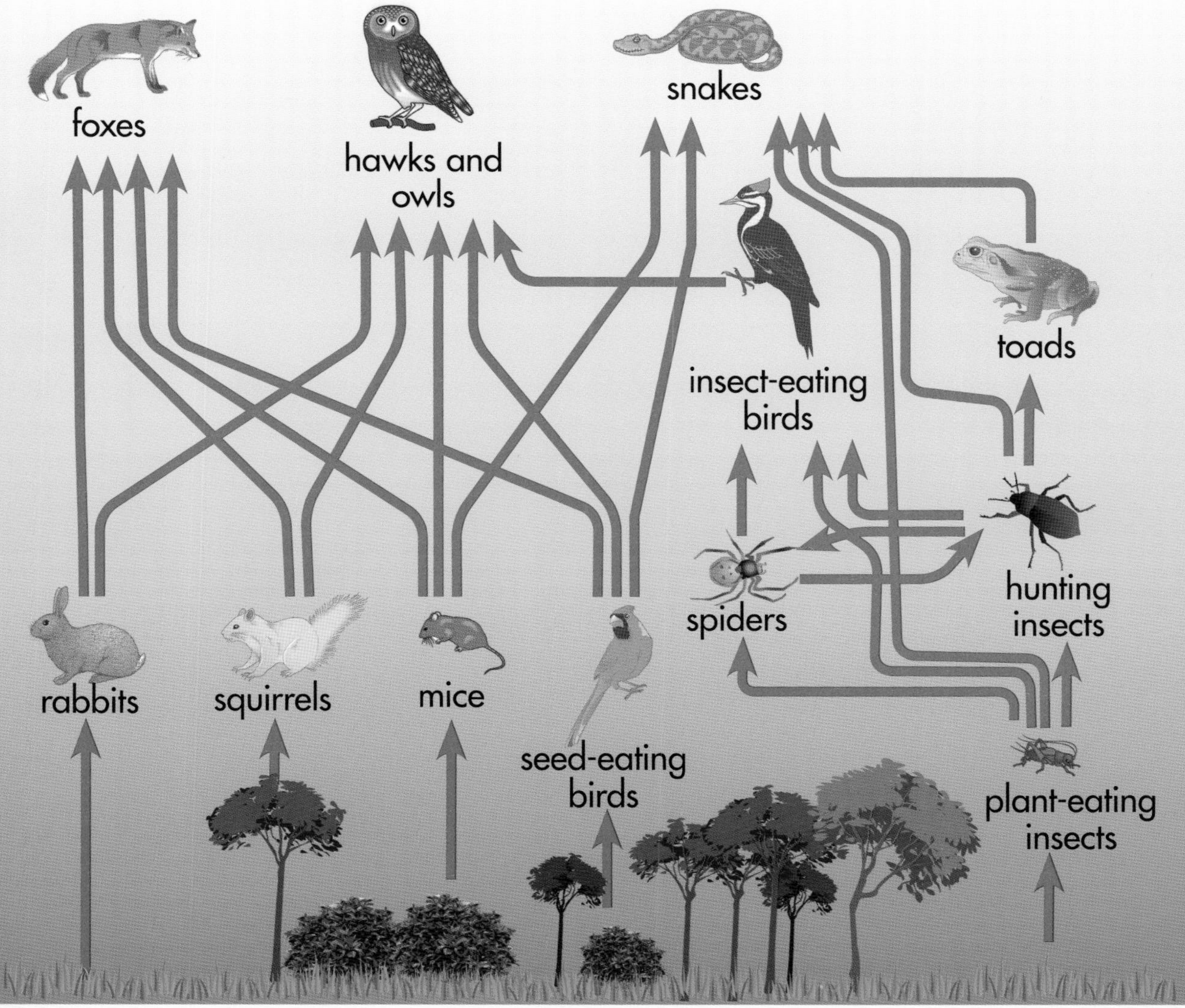
foxes
hawks and owls
snakes
insect-eating birds
toads
spiders
hunting insects
rabbits
squirrels
mice
seed-eating birds
plant-eating insects

LONG JOURNEYS

Many animals make amazingly long journeys to find food and to find places to have their young. These journeys are called **migrations**. This map shows some of the longest migrations.

Pacific salmon
7,020 miles
into the Pacific and back

European eel
3,100 miles
Europe to Sargasso Sea

Arctic tern
43,500 miles
Arctic to Antarctic and back

Green turtle
2,800 miles
Brazil to Ascension Island and back

Gray whale
12,430 miles
Arctic Ocean to Mexican coast and back

ANIMALS IN THE PAST

Many incredible animals were alive in the past, before humans lived on Earth. This infographic is a timeline that shows when some of these animals lived.

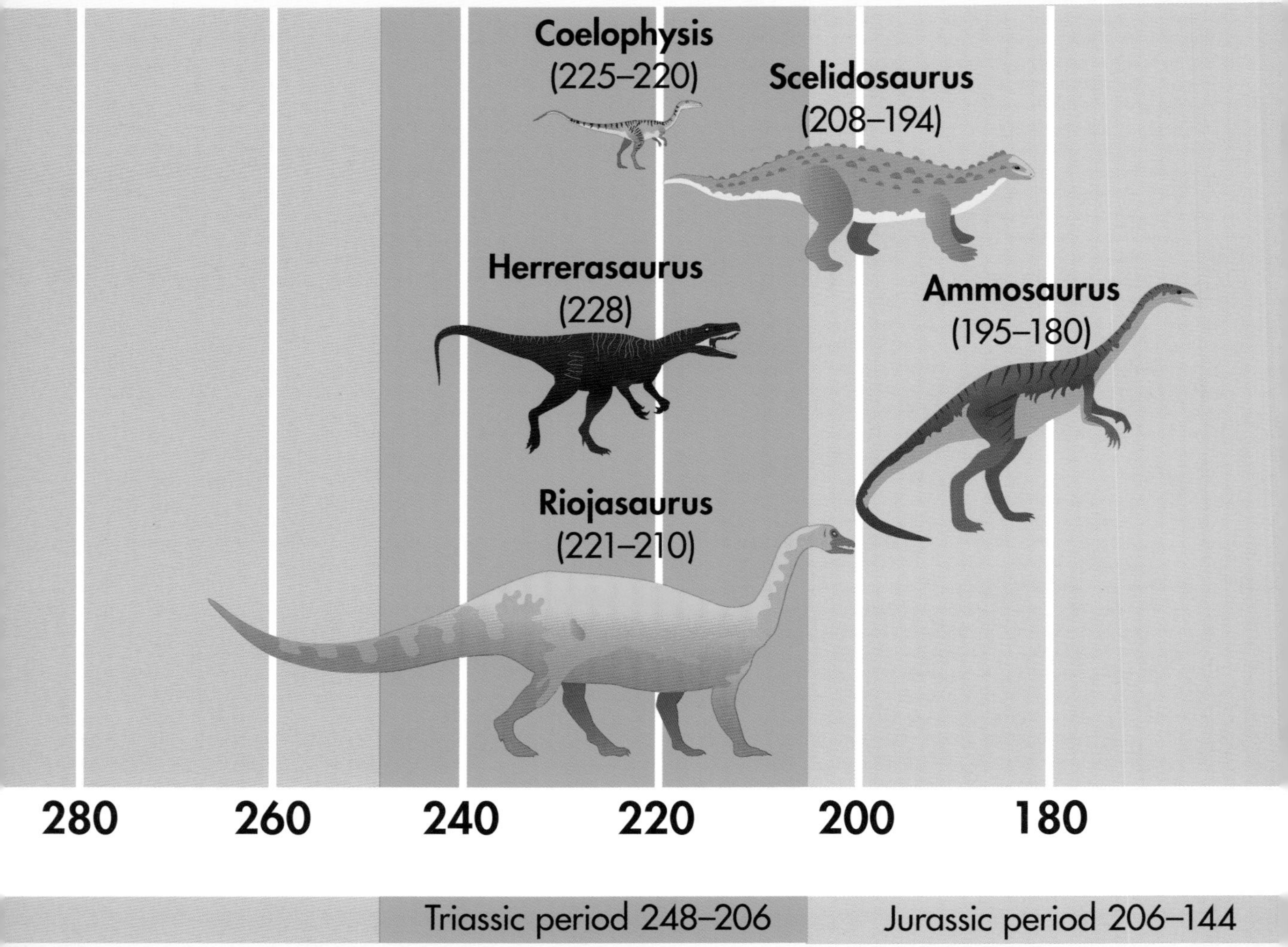

Coelophysis
(225–220)
Scelidosaurus
(208–194)
Herrerasaurus
(228)
Ammosaurus
(195–180)
Riojasaurus
(221–210)
280
260
240
220
200
180
Triassic period 248–206
Jurassic period 206–144

Archaeopteryx
(147)
Megalosaurus
(170–155)
Stegosaurus
(156–140)
Allosaurus
(153–135)
Diplodocus
(155–145)
Velociraptor
(84–80)
Spinosaurus
(95–70)
Tyrannosaurus rex
(67–65)
Giganotosaurus
(112–90)
160
140
120
100
80
60
Million years ago
Cretaceous period 144–65

GLOSSARY

chrysalis hard shell that protects an insect as it changes from a larva to an adult

cicada large flying insect that lives in warm or hot countries

endangered describes an animal that is in danger of dying out

gastrotrich tiny animal that lives in ponds and rivers

krill small shrimp-like animal that lives in the ocean

larva insect before it changes into its adult form. The plural for "larva" is "larvae."

migration long journey from one country or region to another

vaquita small porpoise that lives in the Gulf of California

FIND OUT MORE

Books

Berger, Melvin and Gilda. *101 Animal Records.* New York: Scholastic, 2013.

Bodach, Vijaya. Making Graphs (series). Mankato, Minn.: Capstone, 2008.

McMillan, Dawn. *Understanding Animal Graphs* (Real World Math). Mankato, Minn.: Capstone, 2010.

Web sites

Facthound offers a safe, fun way to find web sites related to this book. All the sites on Facthound have been researched by our staff.
Here's all you do:
Visit www.facthound.com
Type in this code: 9781410962164

INDEX